Carlo Demand

AIRPLANES
OF THE
SECOND WORLD WAR

Coloring Book

Dover Publications, Inc.
New York

Publisher's Note

After the First World War, which saw the sudden and grim development of the airplane from a sportsman's toy to an instrument of death, troupes of barnstormers — trick pilots who performed in fairground after fairground — flew their planes in circles, figure-8's, somersaults, and harrowing dives right into the consciousness of an eager public. The popularity of airplanes increased rapidly: it is estimated that between 1927 and 1932 there were 150 airplane manufacturers in the United States alone. Feats of endurance provided another boost of the plane's reputation. Undoubtedly the most famous such feat was the daring crossing of the Atlantic in 1927 by Charles Lindbergh. Increasingly reliable, faster, and capable of carrying greater and greater loads, the airplane was on its way to becoming what it is today, the world's principal form of long-distance transportation.

Hitler's dream of world conquest spurred the aviation industry to develop increasingly sophisticated aerial weaponry, in Germany and among the future Allies, that would later be used in the Second World War. The technology changed so quickly that many highly effective aircraft of the early years of the war became outdated well before the war's end. Designs ranged from small, wooden, propeller-driven planes to metal jet fighters introduced toward the end of hostilities. Germany developed pilotless rockets, ancestors of today's missiles, that, traveling faster than sound, exploded on English soil before the whine of their flight could be heard. Huge bombers dropped thousands of tons of bombs on every area of combat, devastating Germany and erasing Japan's industrial cities one by one. Among these bombers was the American B-29 "Enola Gay," which dropped the first atomic bomb on Hiroshima, marking the close of an era of warfare.

In his drawings and text Carlo Demand provides a wide range of Second World War aircraft, among them the "Enola Gay," the Japanese Zero used by kamikaze pilots, the German Komet jet fighter, and the spunky British Spitfire that performed so brilliantly in the Battle of Britain and helped to put a stop to Hitler's imperial drive. Some of the depicted aircraft were in use long after war's end. Although all the planes are now obsolete, they played an important role in the evolution of aerial technology, both military and commercial.

The forty-six planes have been illustrated with the colorist in mind and authentic color schemes are detailed in the captions. The artist has rendered thirteen of the planes in color as well; these drawings appear on the covers. Important events and innovations in design are noted in the captions, which provide the reader with general knowledge of Second World War aeronautics.

Copyright

Copyright © 1981 by Dover Publications Inc.
All rights reserved.

Bibliographical Note

Airplanes of the Second World War Coloring Book is a new work, first published by Dover Publications, Inc., in 1981.

International Standard Book Number

ISBN-13: 978-0-486-24107-4
ISBN-10: 0-486-24107-6

Manufactured in the United States by RR Donnelley
24107625   2015
www.doverpublications.com

1. **North American P-51D Mustang, 1944.** One of the best fighters of WWII, the 51-D was the most popular of the Mustangs; 7,956 were built. The depicted aircraft—belonging to the 363rd Fighter Squadron, 357th Fighter Group, 8th Air Force, based in England—had a silver-aluminum finish, a red spinner with a yellow band, and red and yellow checkers on the engine cowling. Top part of the cowling was dark green, the ace-of-clubs insignia white with a green clover leaf, the back part of the rudder red.

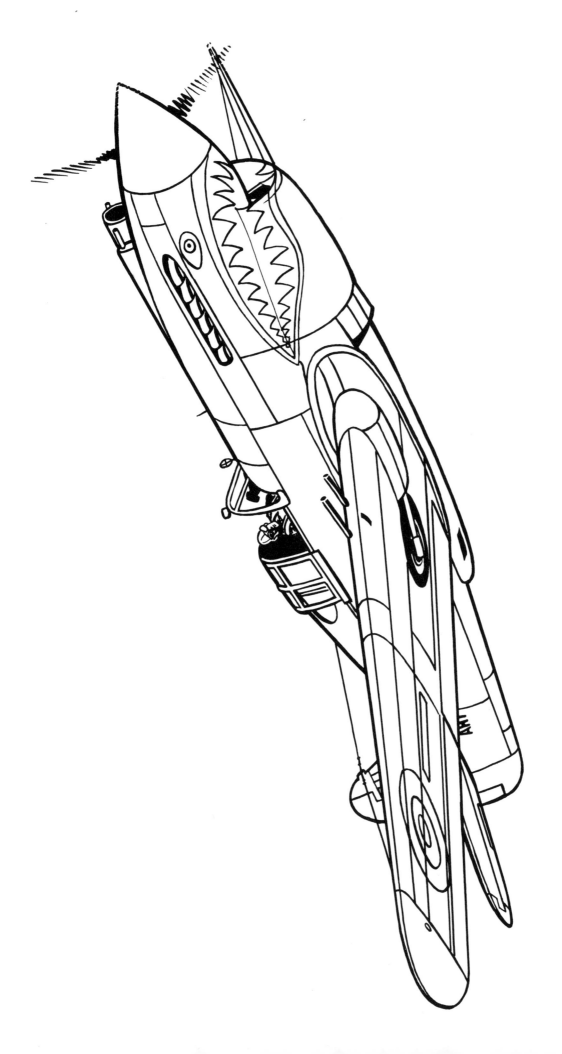

2. Curtiss P-40 Tomahawk, 1941. Named "Warhawk" in the USA, the depicted fighter—originally based at Sidi Haneish with the 112th Squadron, 262nd Wing—was used by the RAF in Egypt. P-40s were supplied to British, French, Chinese, and Russian forces and flown at almost all fronts. Covered with a sand and brown pattern on top, with light blue wing and fuselage undersides. The spinner was red; the shark's mouth was red and blue, the teeth white, the iris red. From outside to inside the wing roundel was blue, white, and red. The rudder flag (front to back) was red, white, and blue.

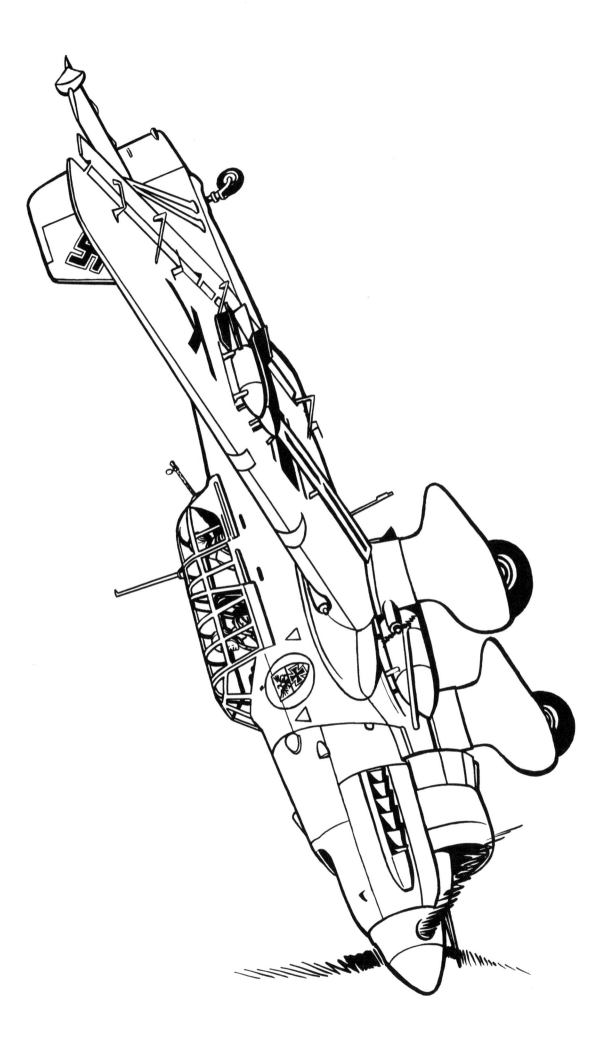

3. **Junkers Ju 87B Stuka, 1940.** The Ju 87 became operational in 1937; the much-improved Ju 87B, part of the Stukageschwader 2 that attacked the RAF base at Tangmere, Sussex, was introduced in 1938. Germany's dark green-gray dive bomber, very successful in the "lightning war" operations, dropped bombs of the same color. Undersides of the wings and fuselage were light blue. The insignia was a yellow circle with a shield, the lower part of which was red around an iron cross. The black swastika was outlined in white.

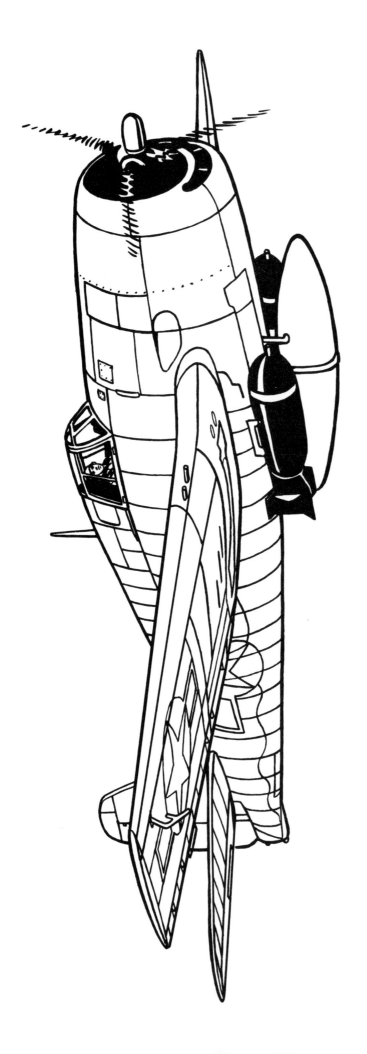

4. Grumman F6F-3 Hellcat, 1944. This American Navy fighter operated with the VF-27 aircraft carrier USS Princeton. Manufactured beginning in 1942, a total of 4,423 planes were produced by April 1944. The highly successful Hellcat was credited with shooting down 5,155 Japanese planes. Fuselage and wings were sea blue on top, light gray underneath. The US insignia — a blue circle with a white star — was set against a white field outlined in blue. The black bombs were ringed in yellow.

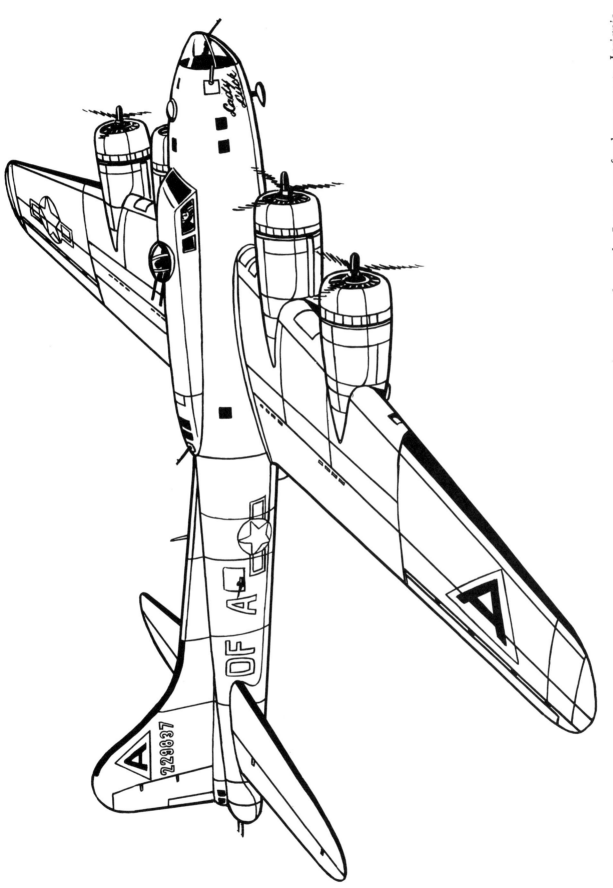

5. Boeing B-17F Flying Fortress, 1942. The most famous American bomber of WWII, the B-17 was used throughout the war. A total of 3,400 model B-17Fs were built after their introduction in the early part of 1942. The depicted B-17F belonged to the 91st Bomb Group, 324th Bomb Squadron, 8th Air Force, Britain. Wings and fuselage olive drab on top, light gray underneath. Letters on fuselage orange. Insignia consisted of a blue circle and a white star and bars outlined in blue. A white triangle and yellow numbers appeared on the red front part of the rudder.

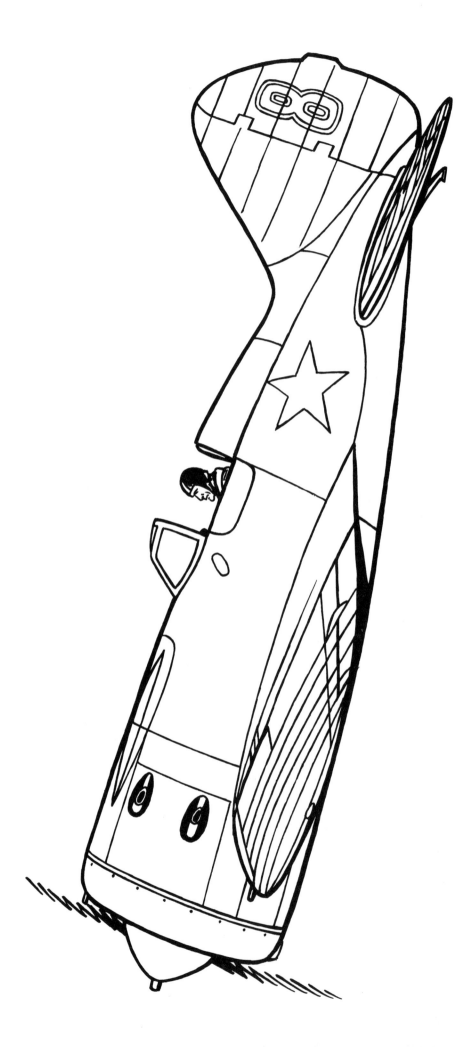

6. **Polikarpov I-16-10 Rata, 1942.** Designed several years before WWII and used in the Spanish Civil War, the I-16 was Russia's most successful fighter, but by 1943 it no longer could match Germany's more advanced fighters. The Rata was superseded by the MiG 3 and the Yak 9. The top was earth brown with a red star, the fuselage underside was pale blue. The yellow number on the rudder was outlined in white.

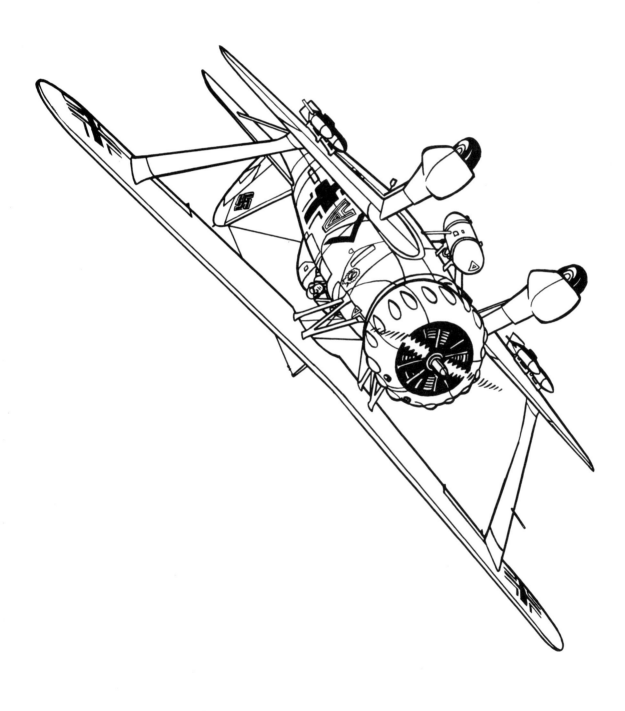

7. Henschel Hs 123-1, 1939. Introduced in 1935, the Hs 123 took part in the Spanish Civil War with the German Legion Condor as a dive bomber. Slow but robust, this plane was used until 1945 for ground attack primarily on the Russian front. The top was green with a darker green pattern, the undersides of the fuselage and wings were light blue.

Landing gear green, bombs dark gray, letter on fuselage red with a white outline. On the rudder a white outline surrounded the black swastika. The cross on the fuselage was black inside, white outside — all of which was outlined in black.

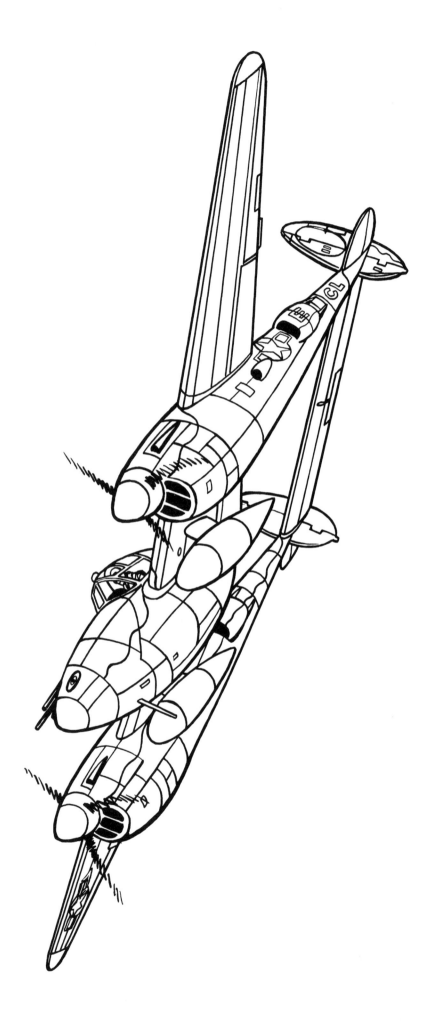

8. Lockheed P-38J-10 Lightning, 1943. Introduced before the war, the P-38 remained in production until 1945, becoming one of WWII's most famous fighters; it was used in every combat area. The P-38J (2,970 were produced) had two 300-gallon drop tanks, enabling it to escort bombers for twelve hours on raids deep into enemy territory.

Fuselage and wings were olive drab on top, pale blue underneath. Insignias had a blue circle and a white star and bars outlined in blue. The letters *E* and *CL* were white, and there was a white circle on the rudder.

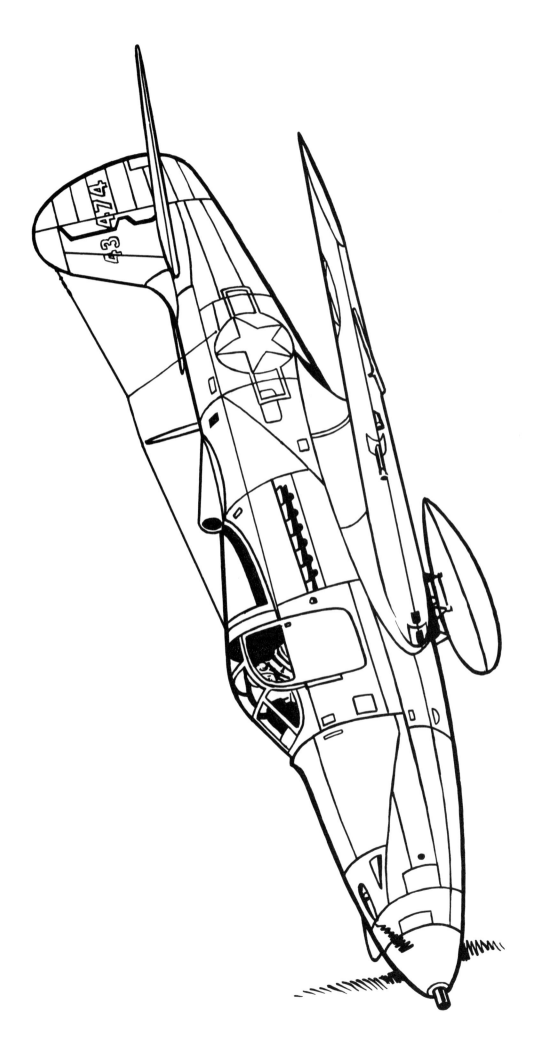

9. Bell P-39Q 20 Be Aircobra, 1943. Mass-produced first in 1939 (eventually 9,558 of the various P-39 models were manufactured), the P-39 was the only fighter with the engine in the middle of the fuselage. Although it was not very successful as a fighter, the P-39 was used in every combat area, and toward the end of 1942 operated successfully in North Africa as a ground attack plane. Sand with a brown pattern on top, the undersides of the wings and fuselage were pale blue.

10. Focke-Wulf Fw 190A-2, 1942. Arguably the best fighter of the German Air Force, the Fw 190A-2 first reached fighter units based at Le Bourget airfield near Paris and saw combat at the Channel coast. While it could not match the Spitfire's turning circle, it outflew its opponent on almost every other count. The depicted aircraft belonged to the 9th Jagdgeschwader 2 stationed at Cherbourg, France in July 1942. Light blue throughout with dark green spots on top of fuselage. Bottom part of engine cowling red. Upper part of wings had a green and dark green pattern. White area around the black cross. The rudder was red, fuselage numbers yellow.

11. **Martin B-26C Marauder, 1944.** A high-speed medium bomber employed in Europe and the Pacific, it first arrived in the UK in February 1943 and aided in the invasion of Europe. Depicted aircraft belonged to the 451st Bombardment Squadron, 322nd Bombardment Group, 9th Air Force, based at Great Saling, UK. Natural metal finish, black and white invasion stripes on fuselage and wings; green, black, and white stripes toward wing tips. Insignias: blue circle and a white star and bars outlined in blue. Inner half of engine cowling green. Rudder, front to back, green and yellow; numerals yellow and green. Green strips in front of letter *E* and after star insignia.

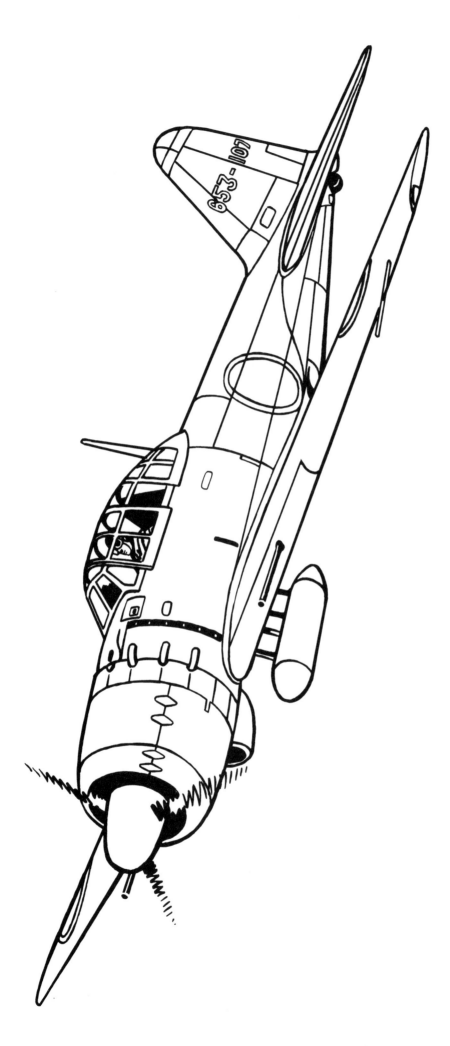

12. Mitsubishi A6M5C Model 52 Zero, 1944. The most famous Japanese fighter of the war, more than 10,000 of all types were built. It was used as a land- or carrier-based fighter, dive bomber, ground attack plane, and as the kamikaze suicide bomber. Fuselage and wings were dark wax green on top, gray underneath. Engine cowling was dark blue, the wings' leading edge was yellow, and the rudder had a yellow stripe at the top with white numerals. Insignia was a red circle with a white outline.

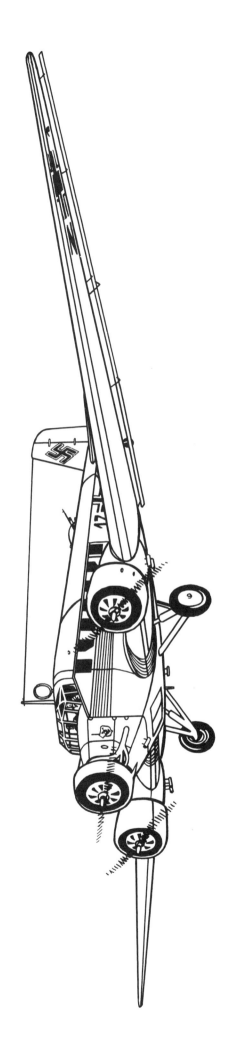

13. Junkers Ju 52/3m, 1941. The most famous German transport of the war, the "Iron Annie," was in service for 30 years, beginning with the flight of a Ju 52ba in 1930. Used throughout the European and African combat zones, the Ju 52 was equipped with three BMW 575 hp 9-cylinder air-cooled radial engines. It was 62 feet long and could carry 10,000 pounds. Wings and fuselage were light blue and green above, light blue below. Yellow appeared on the wings from the tips to the iron cross, on the rudder, and in rings around the engine cowling. Black swastika was outlined in white.

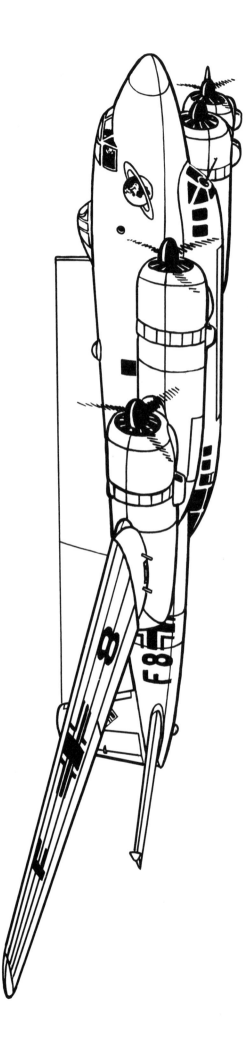

14. Focke-Wulf Fw 200C1 Condor, 1940. Designed as a commercial transport, the Condor established long-distance records before the war, such as flying from Berlin to New York nonstop and returning. Since the German High Command otherwise neglected long-distance heavy bombers, the Condor was the chief reconnaissance bomber during the battle for the Atlantic, striking hundreds of thousands of tons of Allied shipping. Depicted aircraft belonged to the 1st Staffel, KG 40, stationed at Bordeaux, France. The wings and fuselage were light blue underneath, dark green on top. The insignia was a yellow globe encircled by a blue ring.

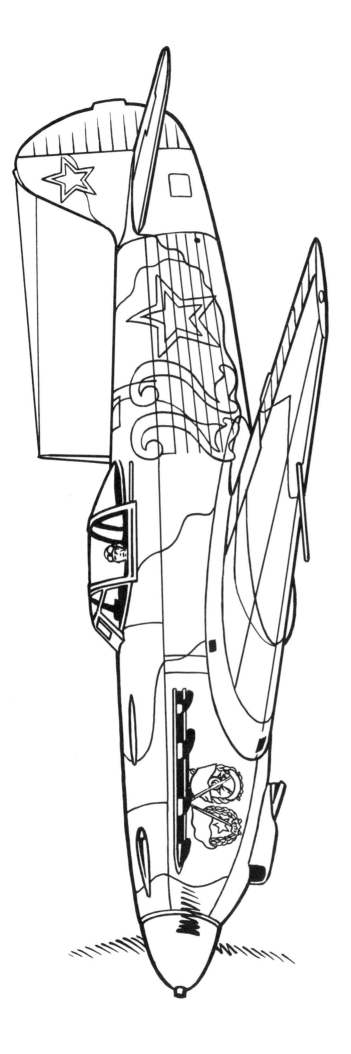

15. Yakolev Yak-9D, 1942. Introduced in 1942, this fighter was the most popular aircraft among Soviet airmen; several thousands were built. Light and simple to maneuver, the Yak-9 performed excellently, sometimes as a ground attack aircraft. Fuselage and wings were covered with a brown and green pattern on top; they were light blue underneath. Beneath the exhaust outlets were insignias with a red flag and star and a yellow wreath. The number was white; behind it was a red star outlined in yellow.

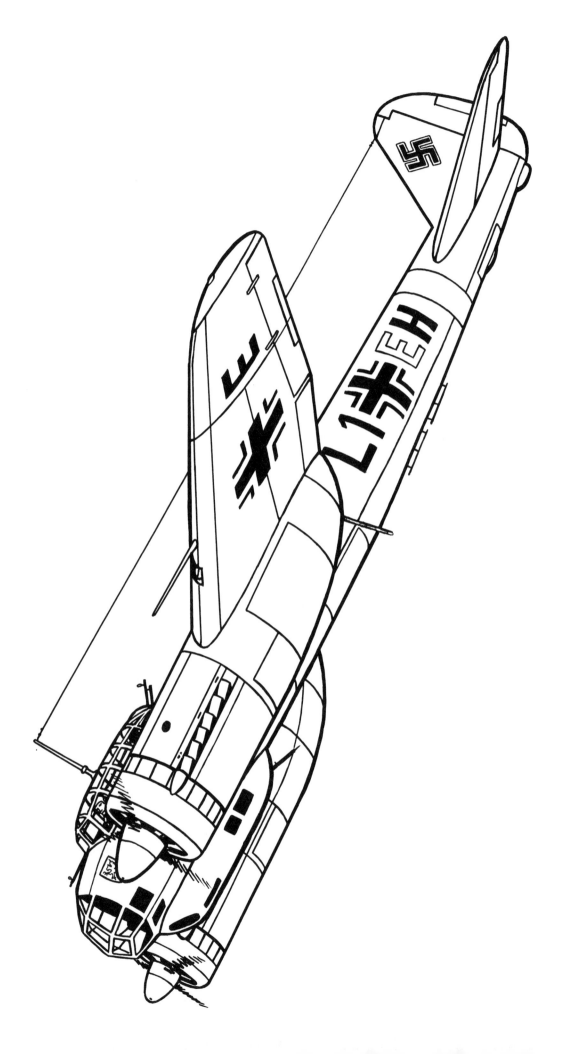

16. Junkers Ju 88A-4 Trop., 1942. Designed in 1935–36 by W. B. Evers and the American Al Gassner, the Ju 88 was produced in great numbers and used on all German fronts. It was utilized as a day or night fighter, medium bomber, torpedo bomber, minelayer, reconnaissance plane, ground attack aircraft, communications aircraft, and, toward the end of the war, as a flying bomb. The aircraft shown here belonged to LG1, based at Benghazi, Libya. Wings and fuselage were sand brown above, light blue below. The white cross was outlined in black; the black swastika was outlined in white. Wing tips were yellow, the spinners black; the letter *E* on the fuselage was white.

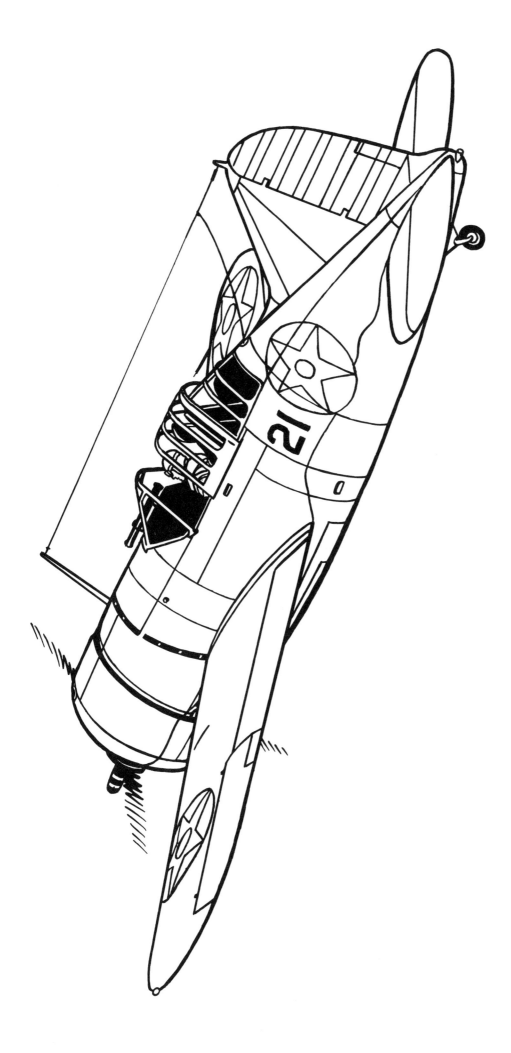

17. Brewster F2A-3 ("Buffalo"), 1942. This small, barrel-shaped American Navy fighter was introduced in 1939 and used by the Finnish Air Force in its war with the Soviet Union. The F2A was exported to Britain (where it was nicknamed "Buffalo"), Belgium, and Holland. The depicted aircraft belonged to the USMC Squadron, VMF-221, based at Ewa, Midway. Fuselage and wings were blue-gray on top, white underneath. The insignia, which appeared on the fuselage and wing, consisted of a white star inscribed in a blue circle with a red dot at its center. The rudder had red and white stripes.

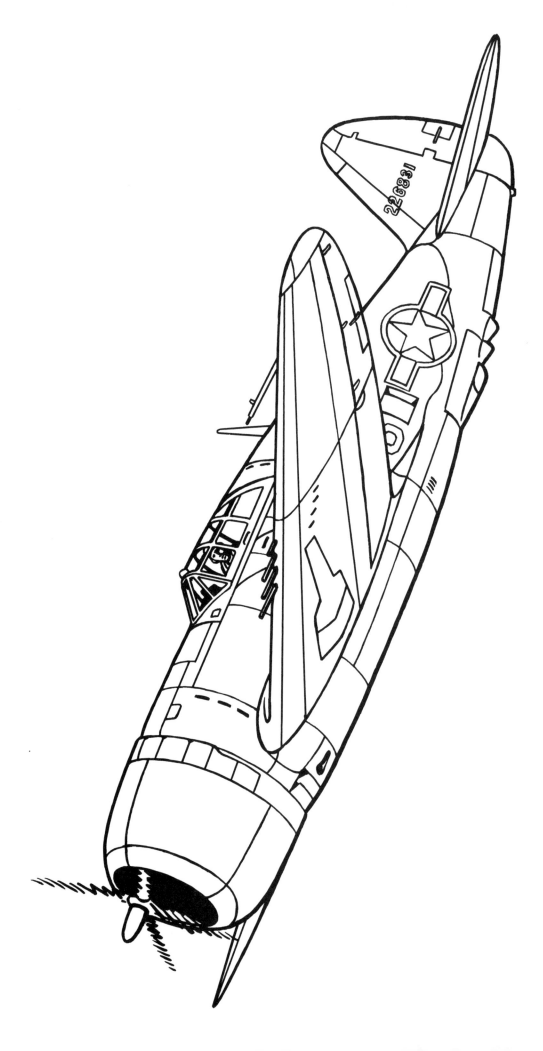

18. Republic P-47D-20 Thunderbolt, 1943. Largest and heaviest single-engine fighter of the war and one of the first aircraft to break the sound barrier in a dive. Armed with eight 12.7 mm machine guns, it was used in Europe and the Pacific. 12,602 model P-47Ds were built. Depicted aircraft belonged to the 324th Fighter Group, 12th Air Force, in Italy. Wings and fuselage olive drab above, gray below. Yellow for the cowl and fuselage stripes and rudder numerals. Insignia: a blue circle and a white star and bars outlined in red. Natural metal finish for the canopy frame.

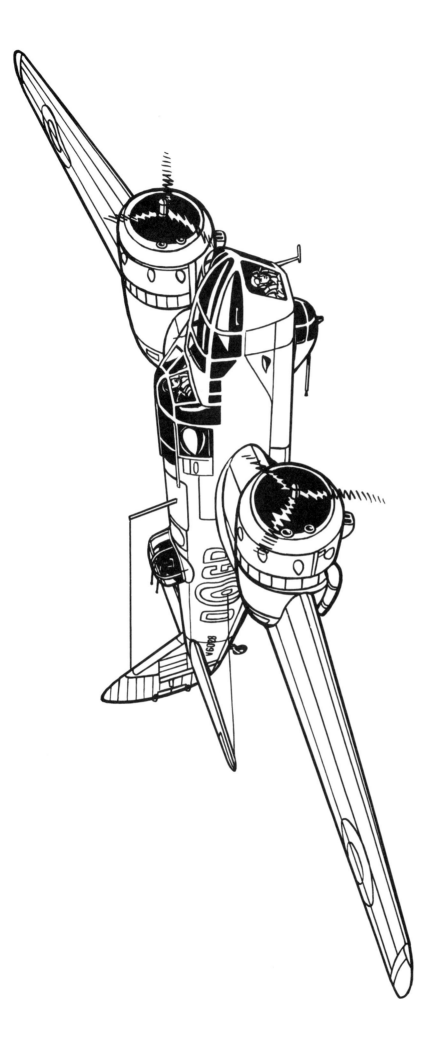

19. **Bristol Blenheim Mk. IV, 1941.** Fast and maneuverable British medium bomber of first war years. 1,930 were built. Used in first bombing mission at Schilling Roads, near Wilhelmshaven, but suffered heavy losses during German advance into Holland, Belgium, and northern France. By 1942 most were replaced by Bostons and Mosquitoes. Wings and fuselage camouflaged dark earth and dark green; underside light blue-green. Fuselage roundels (inside to outside) red, white, blue, and yellow. Red and blue roundels on wings. Rudder flag (front to back) red, white, and blue. Letter pale gray.

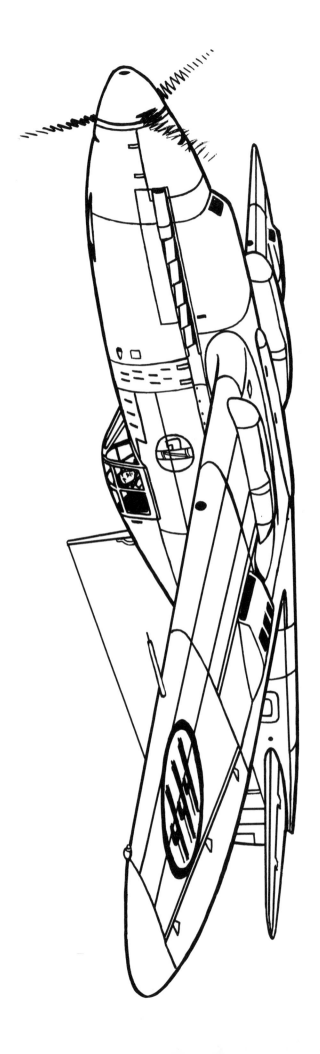

20. Caproni Reggiana Re 2001 Falco II, 1942. An excellent Italian single-seat fighter introduced in 1940, but deliveries of the Alfa Romeo–built Daimler-Benz DB 601 A engines could not meet the demand. The depicted aircraft was with the 150 Squadriglia, 2nd Gruppo Caccia Terrestre, 6th Stormo, based in Ravenna. Fuselage and wings earth brown on top, light gray underneath. The front part of the cowl up to the first exhaust stump was yellow. Fuselage insignia: a blue circle, light brown bundle, and a white ax handle. Vertical bar on rudder was white, fuselage numerals gray.

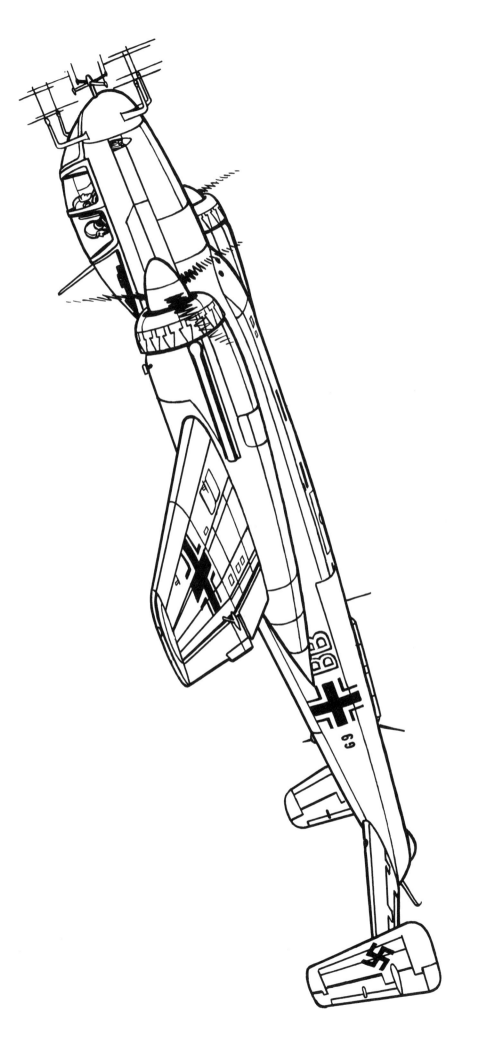

21. Heinkel He 219 A-O Uhu, 1944. Originally designed as a long-range reconnaissance aircraft, the "Uhu-owl" became a heavy night fighter. Prior to August 1943, when full production began, only 268 planes had been manufactured. The 219s had good flying qualities and could have played a larger role in the war if political differences among the German leaders had been resolved. The aircraft shown here belonged to the Gruppenstab I./N.J.1 and was equipped with FuG 220a Lichtenstein SN2 airborne radar. Gray throughout, it had a small blue and red badge under the cockpit, black crosses and swastikas, and two B's — the first black, the second red — on the fuselage side.

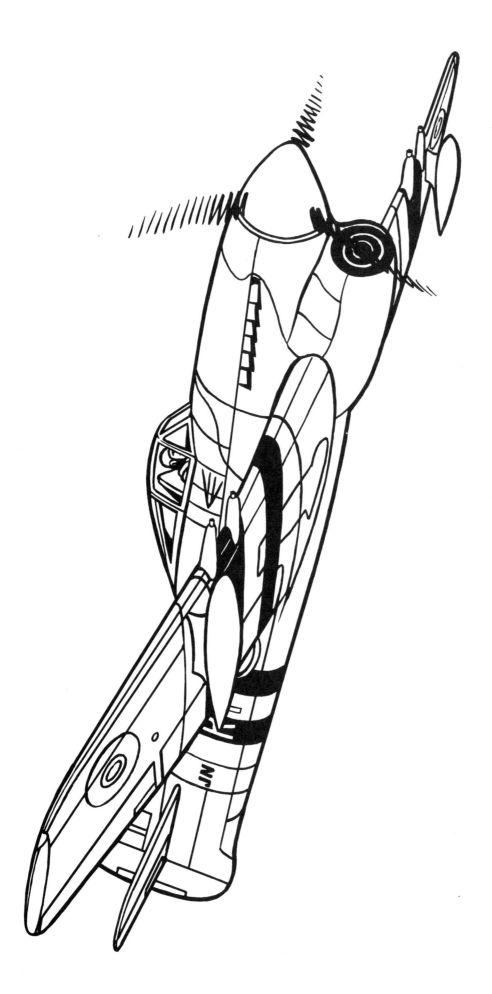

22. Hawker Tempest V-1, 1944. One of the war's finest ground attack aircrafts, the Tempest was employed by front-line outfits from January 1944. 805 Tempest Vs were built. The Tempest operated over the English Channel and southern England and proved to be a very successful train killer, but its specialty was shooting down German V-1s: 648 buzz bombs fell to the Tempests. Wings and fuselage camouflaged with earth brown on top; undersides pale gray. Wing roundel (inside to outside) was red, white, and blue. Fuselage and wing stripes were black and white. Rudder flag (front to back) was red, white, and blue. Fuselage roundel ringed in yellow. White and gray letters.

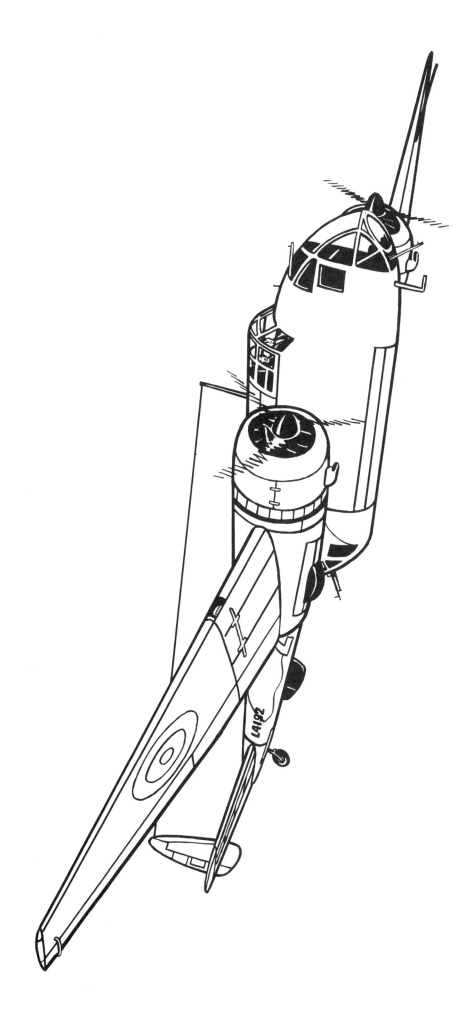

23. Handley Page Hampden Mk. I, 1940. This British medium bomber was introduced to the RAF in 1938 and was one of its main bombers at the beginning of the war; eight RAF squadrons were equipped with it. The Hampden was poorly armed, however, and suffered great losses during the first two years of the war. Later it proved to be more successful as a night bomber over Germany and the Low Countries. The entire aircraft was camouflaged with an earth and green pattern except for the undersides of the wings and fuselage, which were black. The roundel (inside to outside) was red, white, and blue.

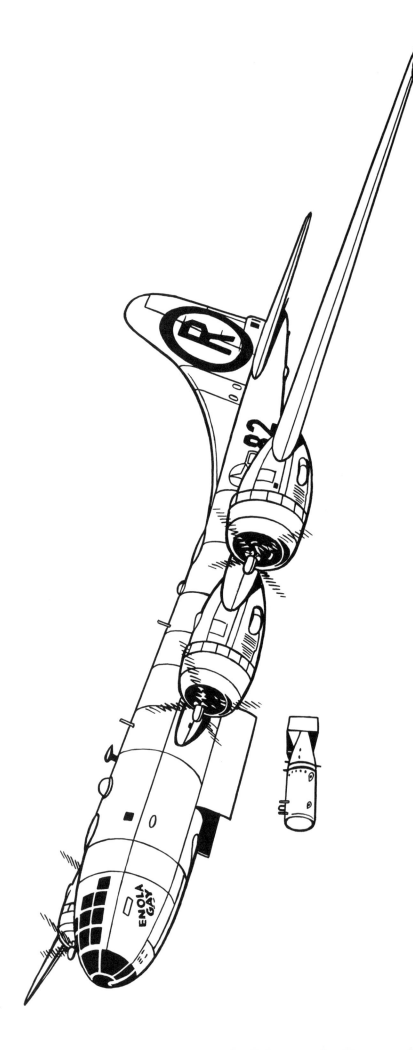

24. Boeing B-29 Superfortress, 1945. The Superfortress played a major role in the Pacific, where it served as a minelayer around Japan and was used systematically by the American 20th Air Force to erase Japanese industrial cities one by one. Pictured here is the "Enola Gay," which dropped the first atomic bomb on Hiroshima on 6 August 1945.

A B-29 also delivered the second atomic bomb on Nagasaki, which effectively ended the war. Natural metal finish covered the entire plane. National insignia: blue circle with a white star and bars outlined in blue. Yellow square between name and cockpit windows. Bombs olive drab.

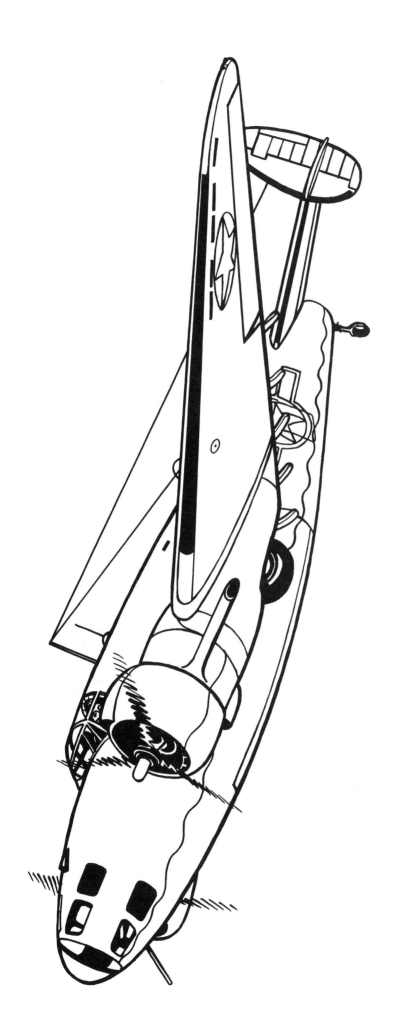

25. Lockheed A-28 Hudson I, 1939. Developed from the civilian model 14, the RAF received the first 350 Hudsons in 1938. Hudsons were employed by the American, British, Canadian, Australian, New Zealand, Dutch, and Chinese air forces. An RAF 224th Squadron Hudson was the first English aircraft to shoot down a German plane, a Dornier D 18 on 8 October 1939. Many Hudsons were used by the Coastal Command for sea reconnaissance and U-boat hunting. Wings and fuselage olive drab on top, pale gray underneath. National insignia on fuselage: white star and bar on a dark blue circle, all outlined in red. Wing insignia: dark blue circle with white star.

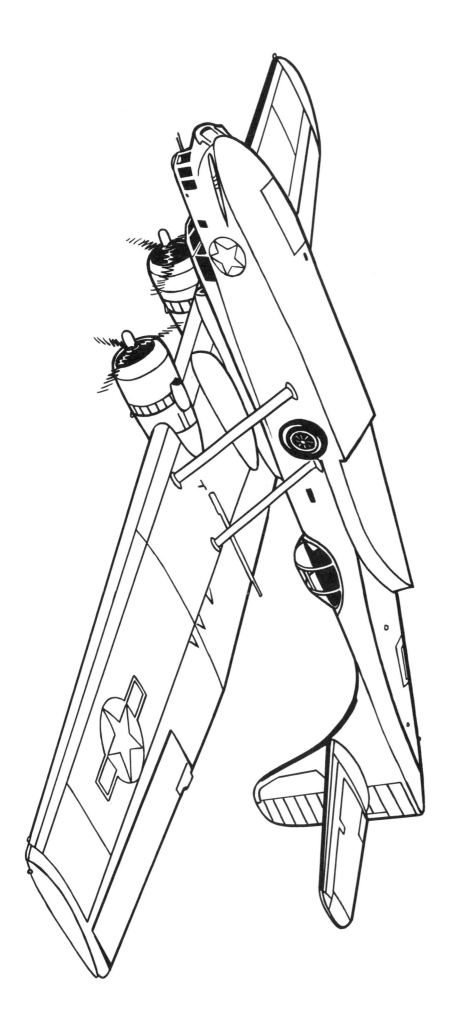

26. Consolidated PBY-6A Catalina, 1944. One of the most famous aircraft of the time, the PBY (named "Catalina" by the British, who ordered 650) was first flown in 1935 and proved useful for many tasks: as a bomber, torpedo carrier, sea reconnaissance aircraft, ship convoy escort, mail and freight plane, and submarine hunter. The US Navy ordered the "Cat" in 1936. Sea blue on top with a pale gray underside, the Catalina had one insignia – dark blue circle, white star – on the fuselage and another – dark blue circle, white star, white bar outlined in dark blue – on the wing.

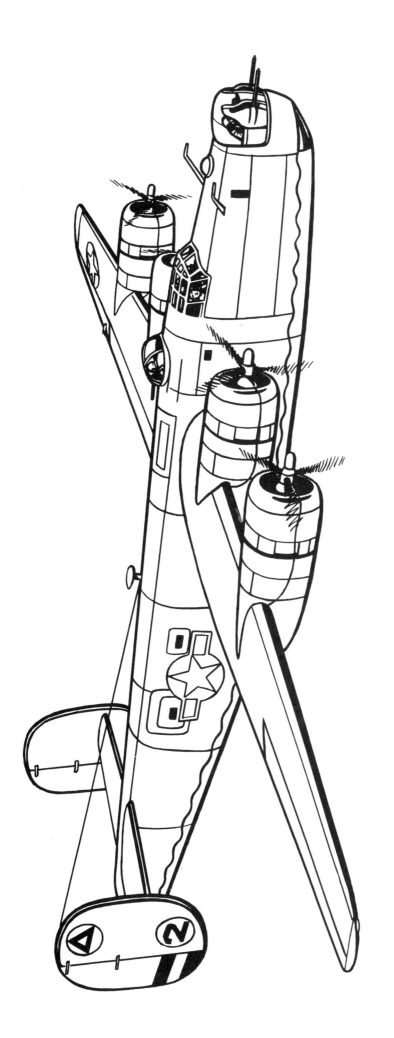

27. Consolidated B-24J Liberator, 1943. A successful and reliable heavy bomber, reconnaissance aircraft, and submarine bomber, it was also used as a VIP transport and ferried pilots and personnel across the North Atlantic. Produced in large numbers, Liberators dropped more than 635,000 tons of bombs on Europe, Africa, and the Pacific, and shot down 4,189 enemy aircraft. Dark olive drab on top, pale gray underneath. Fuselage insignia: dark blue circle and a white star and bars outlined in dark blue. Wing insignia: blue circle and white star. On the rudder were black and white stripes and two white circles, one with a black triangle, the other with a black number 2.

28. Avro Lancaster B.I, 1944. The Lancaster, Britain's most famous heavy bomber, was first flown on 9 January 1941; it flew its first bombing mission into Germany in 1942. Used for air raids for many years, it was equipped with special dambuster bombs for its two attacks in 1943 on German water reservoir dams. The depicted aircraft belonged to the No. 150 Squadron, based at Hemswell, Lincs. Camouflage pattern of light brown and green on top. Black on fuselage sides and undersides. Wing roundels red and blue; fuselage roundels (inside to outside) red, white, blue, and yellow. Red letters. Rudder flag (left to right) was red, white, and blue.

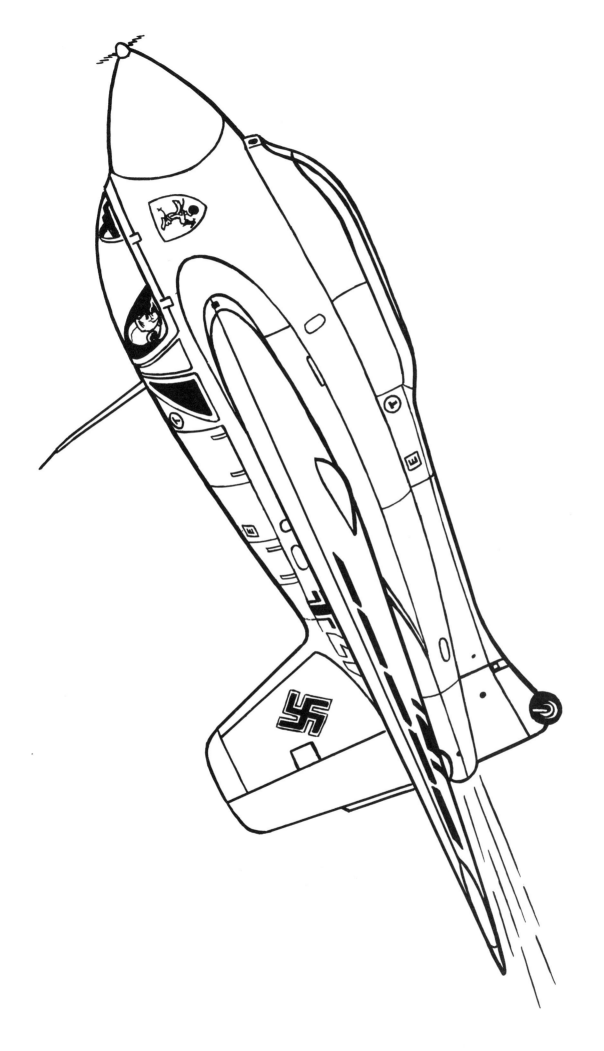

29. Messerschmitt Me 163-B-1 Komet, 1944. The first rocket-powered fighter, the Komet could fly at 596 mph at 30,000 feet, making it one of the fastest aircraft of the decade. Its small size and limited range (it could fly for only ten minutes at full power) suited it for defensive missions against Allied bombers. 350 were built. The depicted aircraft was with the 2nd JG 400 at Brandis, Germany. Camouflage pattern of green and dark green on top; underside light blue. Black swastika outlined in white, fuselage number white, the *E* and *T* fuel caps yellow. Badge had a red-coated figure set against a blue ground.

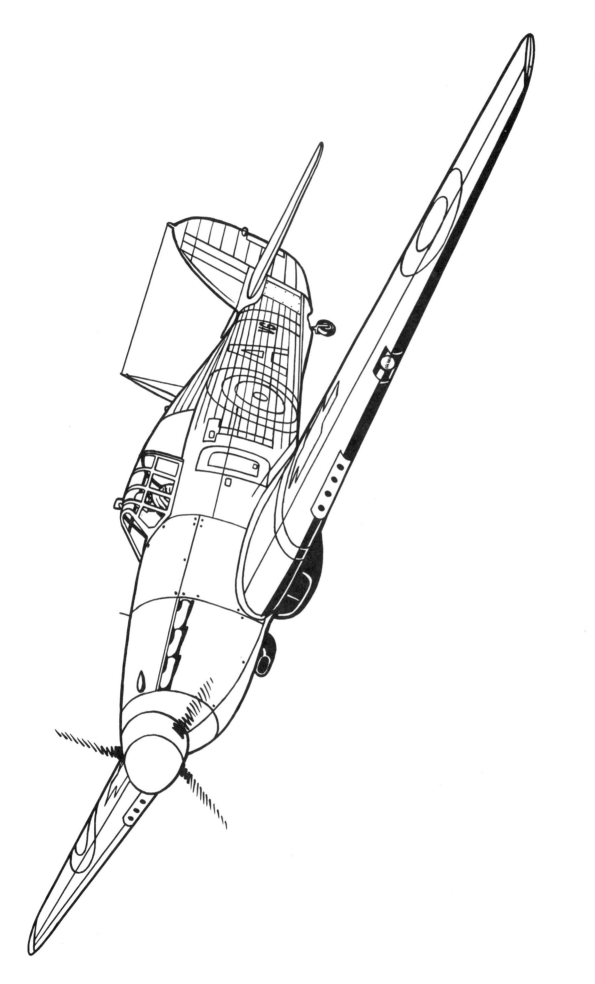

30. Hawker Hurricane Mk. I, 1940. Britain's most modern fighter at the outbreak of the war and the only British fighter to exceed 300 mph in level flight, it carried the heaviest burden in the Battle of Britain. Over three-fifths of the RAF's planes were Hurricanes. Also used as a convoy escort plane and a light bomber in North Africa. Depicted aircraft belonged to the 257th Fighter Squadron, North Weald, England. Sand brown and green camouflage pattern on top, underside pale gray. Red spinner; black exhaust pipes; fuselage roundel (inside to outside) red, white, blue, and yellow. Rudder flag (front to back) red, white, and blue. Gray letters. Wing roundels blue and red.

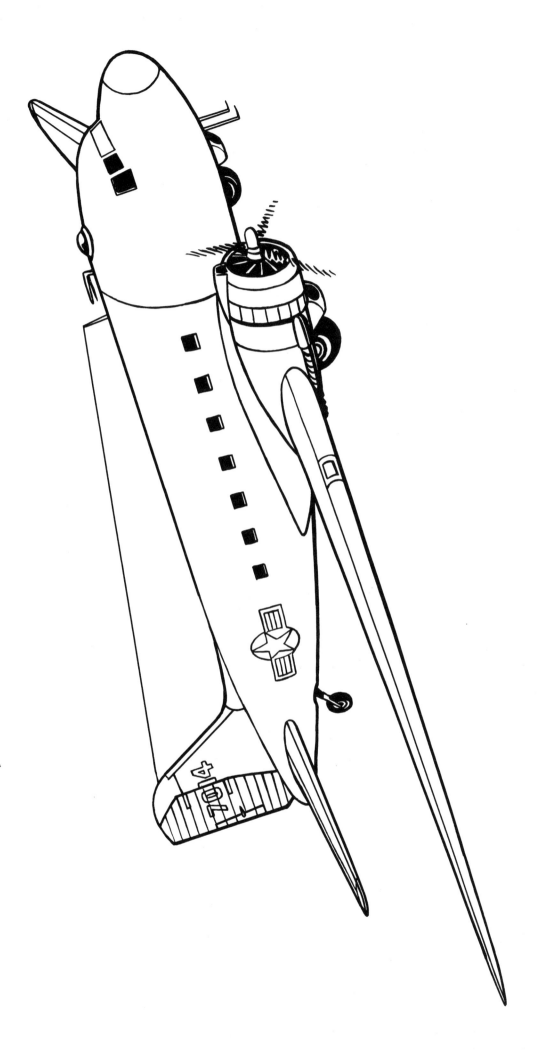

31. Douglas C-47A, 1942. No aircraft of the US Army Air Force has been more widely known and saw more service than the "Gooney Bird." Produced in greater numbers than any other transport, the C-47 served in every combat area of the war as a troop transport, freight plane, and tow plane for troop carriers. Over 10,000 C-47s of all types have been built, including the DC-3, the commercial version, which was used for many years after the war. Olive drab on top, pale gray underneath. National insignia — white star, blue circle, white bars outlined in dark blue, with red stripes in center of bars — on fuselage. Rudder numerals yellow.

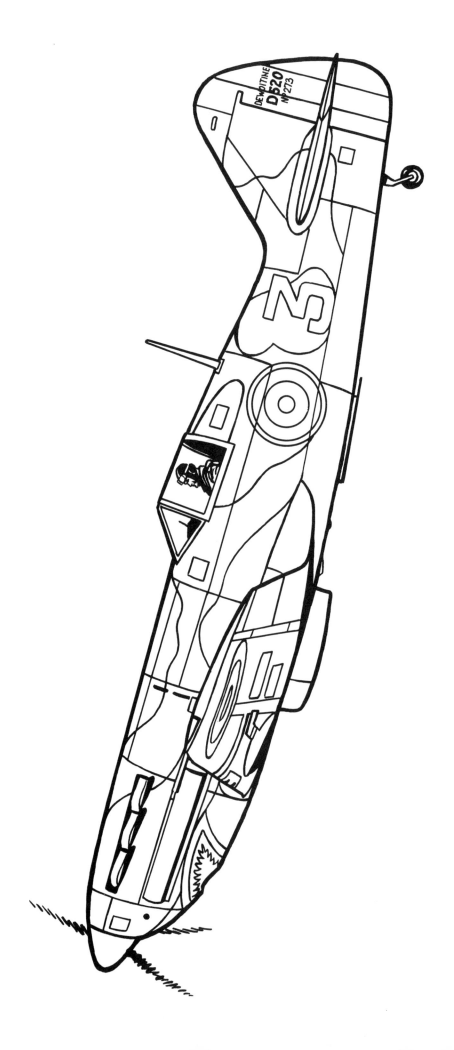

32. **Dewoitine 520, 1940.** Produced at the beginning of hostilities in 1939, the 520 was delivered to the French Air Force later that year and proved to be France's best fighter in the battle of France in 1940. After the French defeat, German authorities permitted the production of the plane for the Vichy government, which brought the total number of 520s, including those used by the German Air Force, to 600. Blue-gray and green camouflage pattern on top, bottom light blue. Roundels (inside to outside) blue, white, red, and yellow. The shark mouth and lips were red, the teeth white. Fuselage number was white.

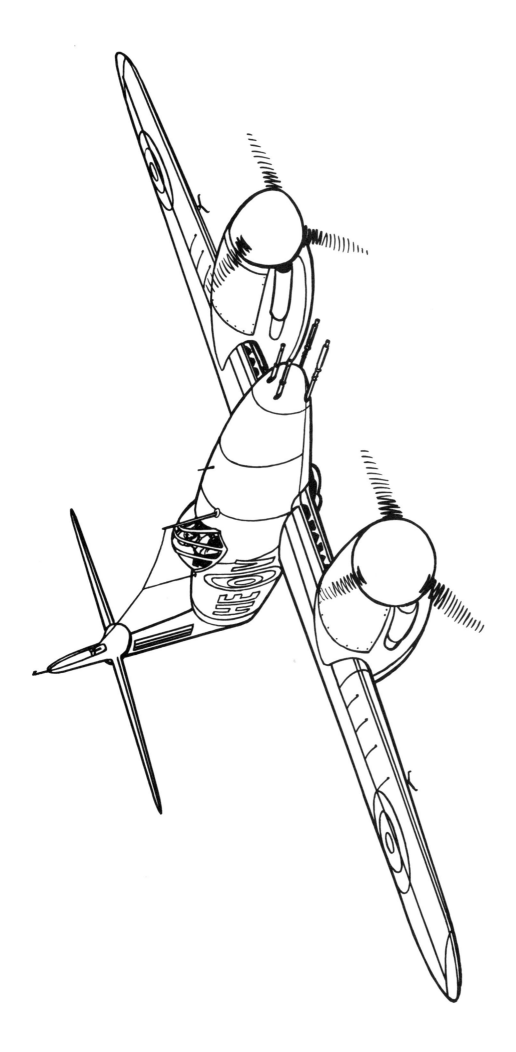

33. **Westland Whirlwind F.Mk.I, 1941.** First flown in 1938, the Whirlwind was delivered in 1940 to the RAF, which employed it successfully as a ground attack aircraft and long-range fighter escorting bombers into enemy territory. A pattern of bluish sea-green and green covered the top of the aircraft; the underside was light blue. Fuselage roundel (inside to outside) was red, white, blue, and yellow; wing roundels were red, white, and blue. Letters and spinners were white, the rudder flag (front to back) red, white, and blue.

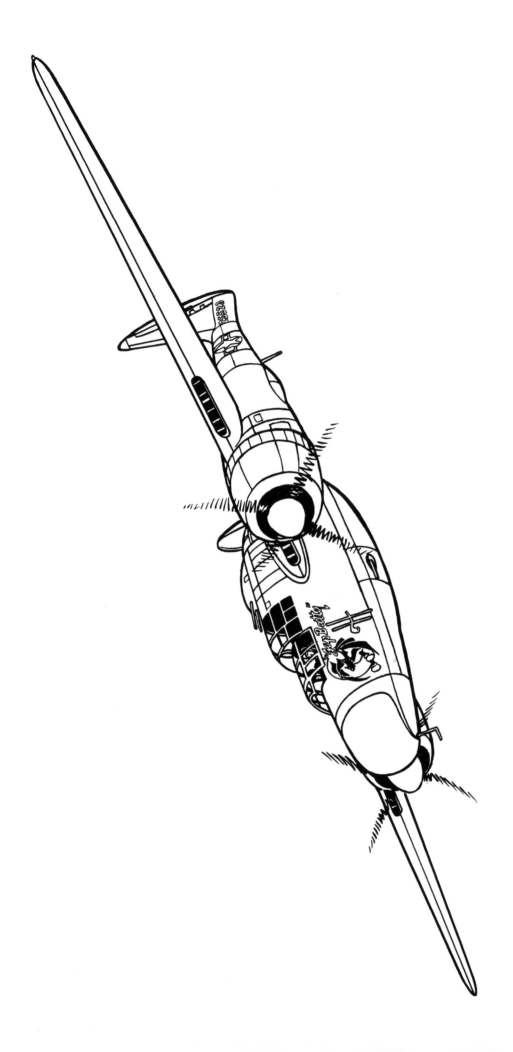

34. Northrop P-61 A-1 Black Widow, 1944. The first aircraft designed as a night fighter, though some were used for reconnaissance. Not flown until 1942, by summer 1944 it was operating in Europe and the Pacific. Equipped with radar, four 20 mm cannons, and four heavy machine guns. The P-61 A pictured here belonged to the 6th NFS based at Saipan. Olive drab on top, underside pale gray. Insignia: blue circle and a white star and bars outlined in blue. Three white and two black bands extended from under the insignia to center line of fuselage. Fuselage nose white, numbers yellow. Each wing had two black and three white bands. Badge: white circle with red bat and yellow shoes. Yellow letters.

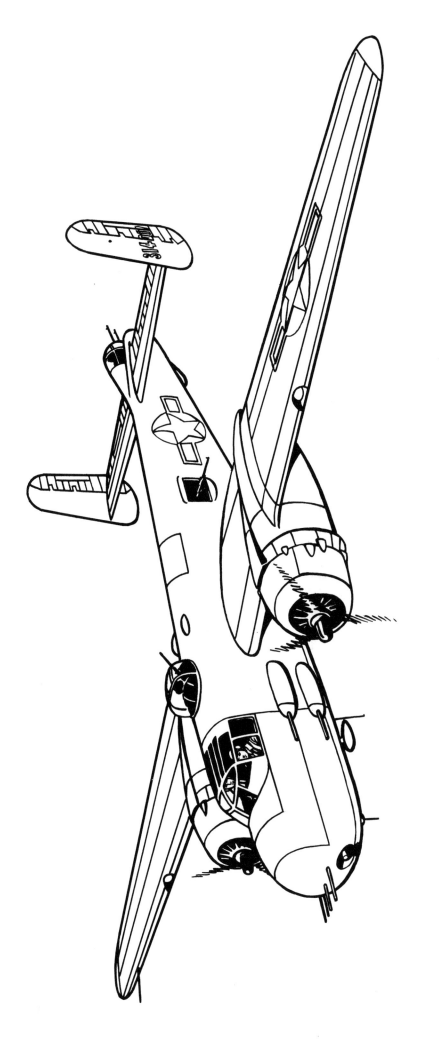

35. North American B-25G Mitchell, 1944. Introduced by the Army Air Force in 1941, over 5,000 B-25s of all types were built. The Soviet Union received 75 in March 1942, the first delivery of what would ultimately total 850 planes. The plane was also used by Dutch, Brazilian, and Canadian forces. The US Navy adapted the B-25 to serve as a submarine hunter. The model B-25G pictured here was equipped with additional guns on the side of the fuselage below the cockpit. Olive drab on top; pale gray undersides. National insignia: dark blue circle and a white star and bars outlined in dark blue. Rudder numerals white.

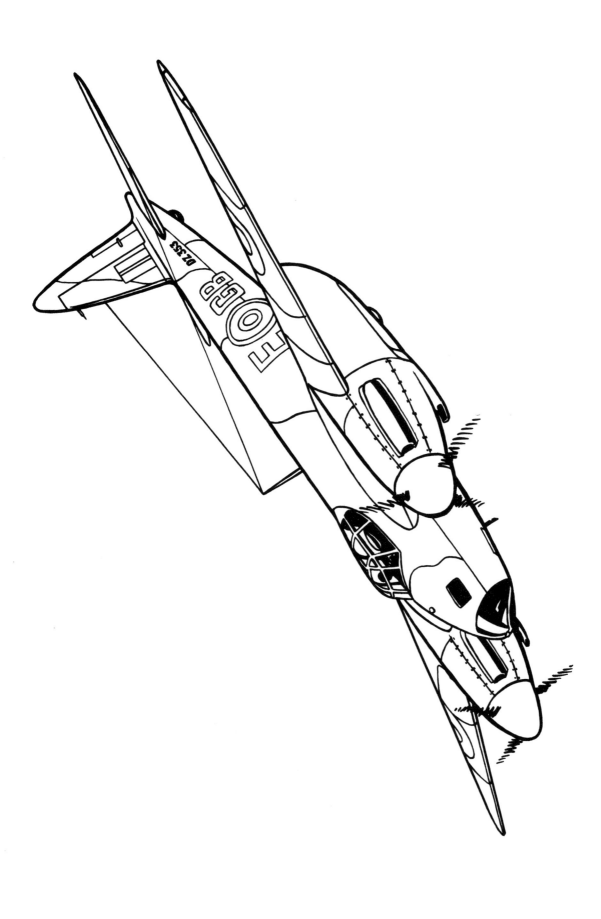

36. de Havilland Mosquito Mk. IV, 1943. The number manufactured —7,781 of all types—attests that the all-purpose Mosquito was one of the finest planes of the war. Constructed mainly of wood (and nicknamed "Wooden Wonder"), it was used from 1941 as a day and night fighter and bomber, ground attack aircraft, photoreconnaissance plane, transport, trainer, and ship killer. The pictured Mosquito belonged to the No. 105th Squadron (B) stationed at Horsham and Marham, St. Faith, England. Sea-green and light brown pattern on top, light gray underneath. Wing roundels blue and red; fuselage roundels (inside to outside) red, white, blue, and yellow. White letters.

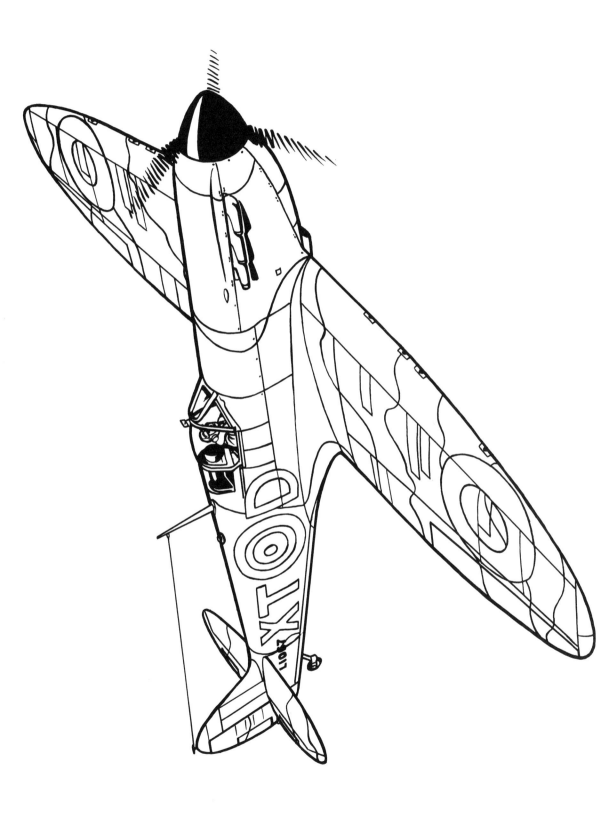

37. Supermarine Spitfire Mk. Ia, 1940. England's most famous fighter, the Spitfire made a brilliant showing in the Battle of Britain. More Spitfires of all types were produced than any other British aircraft until 1947; the total was over 20,000. The Spitfire shown here belonged to the No. 603 "City of Edinburgh" Squadron, based at Dyce,

England. A camouflage pattern of earth, light brown, and green on top; light gray underneath. Spinner and exhaust pipes black; white letters; rudder flag (front to back) red, white and blue. Wing roundels red and blue; fuselage roundel (inside to outside) red, white, blue, and yellow.

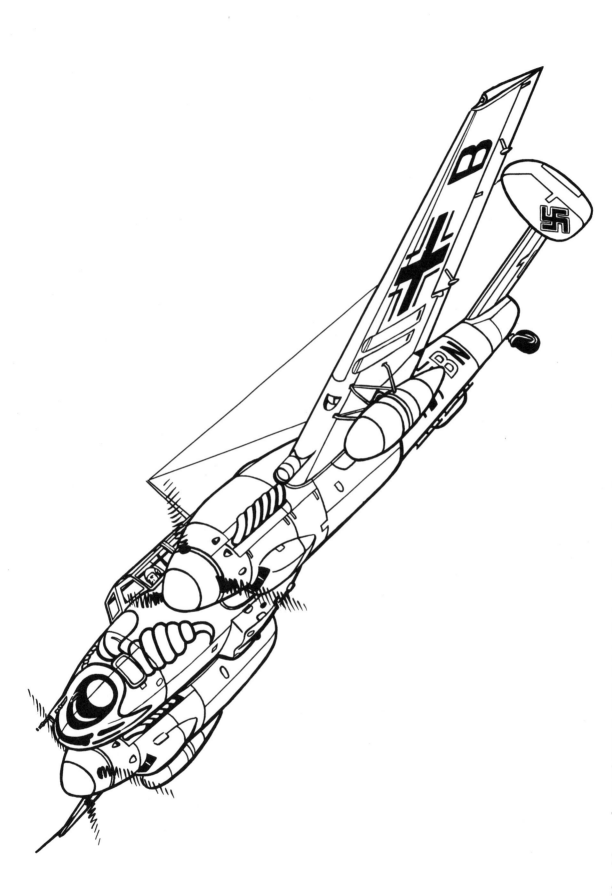

38. Messerschmitt Bf 110G-2, 1943. Originally intended as a day and night fighter, it developed into an all-purpose aircraft, first seeing combat in 1939 in Poland, where it was used as a low-level ground attack aircraft. Used toward the end of the war as a night fighter and reconnaissance aircraft. Depicted aircraft belonged to the II./ZG (destroyer) 1 "Wasp" stationed in Italy. Light blue-gray with green spots that got thicker toward the top of the fuselage. Green and light green camouflage pattern on wings. Spinners black with red tip, wing cross black with white and black outlines, fuselage letters red and black. Black swastika outlined in white. White ring around fuselage behind the letter *N.* Wasp's body yellow with a red curve in eye. Eyeball white.

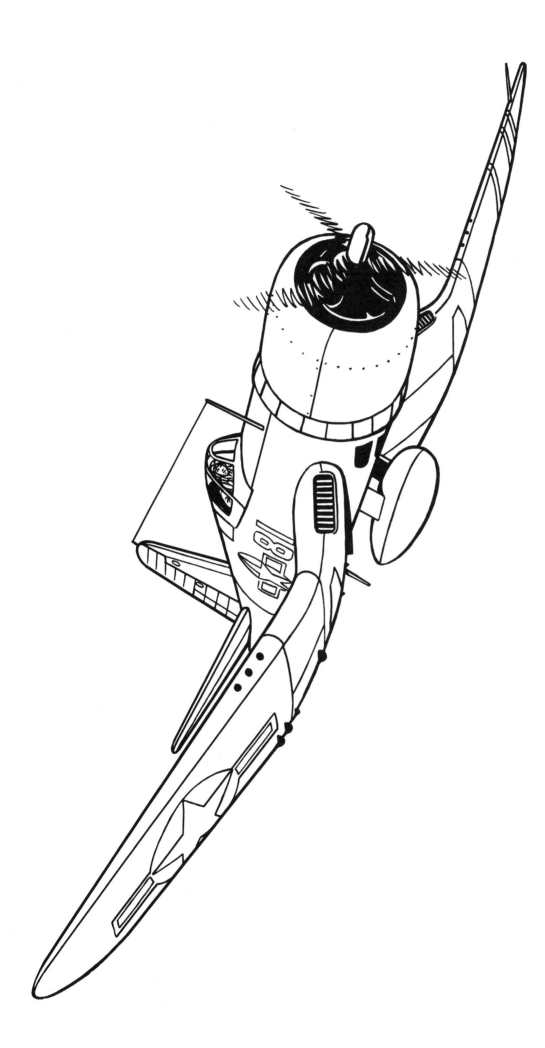

39. Chance Vought F4U-1 Corsair, 1945. The Corsair, the Navy's strongest carrier fighter, was used during the latter half of the war in the Pacific. The different versions of the plane (12,681 of all types were produced) were credited with shooting down over 2,000 Japanese aircraft. The Corsair was also often used as a ground-attack aircraft. Navy blue except for the light gray underside, the Corsair bore the dark blue circle and white star and bars outlined in blue of the national insignia. Fuselage number white.

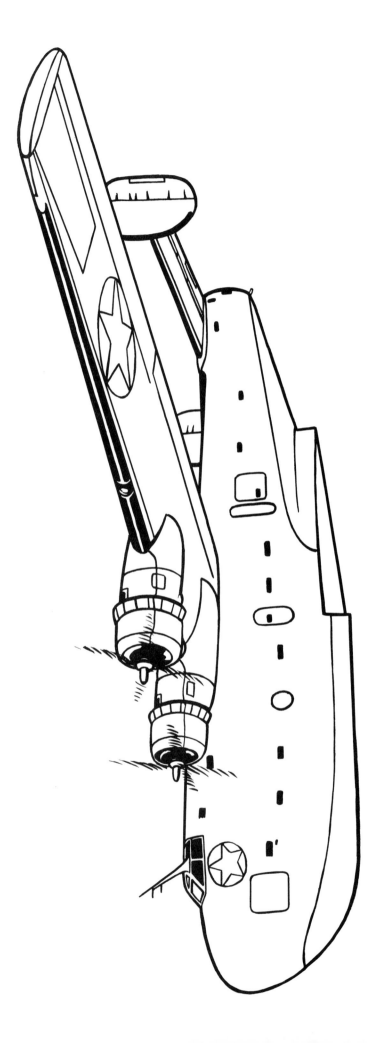

40. Consolidated PB2Y-3R Coronado, 1944. First flown in 1937 as a patrol bomber. The Navy received its first Coronado in 1941 and used the flying boat for many different missions. Its main role was as a long-range transport; it was used as a hospital transport as well (it carried 25 stretchers on board). The bomber version had a crew of 10, the transport 5. Powered by 1,200 hp Pratt and Whitney-1830-88 Twin Wasp double radial engines, Coronadoes were used as transatlantic transports in 1944. Wings and fuselage navy blue with pale gray undersides. The national insignias consisted of white stars on dark blue circles.

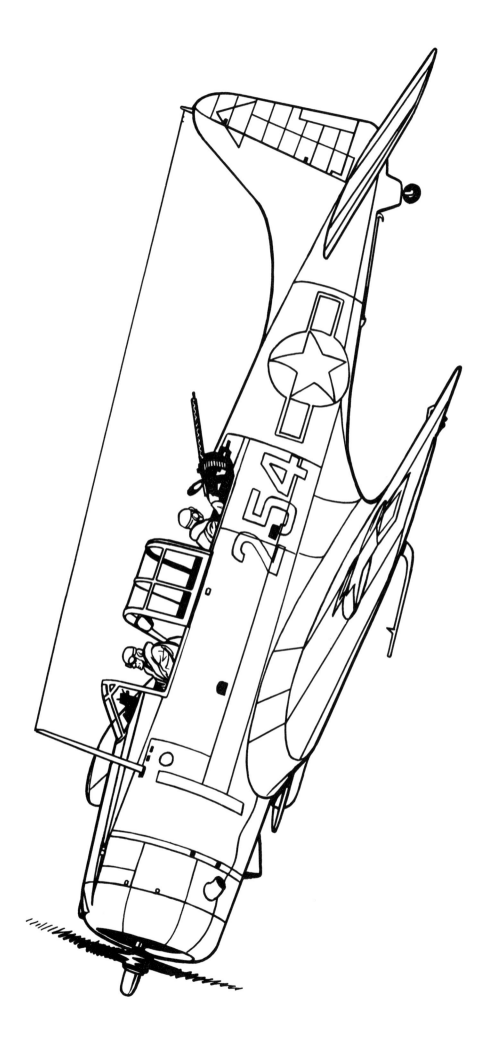

41. Douglas SBD Dauntless, 1941. Already outdated at the time of the Japanese attack on Pearl Harbor, the Dauntless nevertheless bore the brunt of aerial warfare in the Pacific until more sophisticated aircraft arrived. The 5,936 Dauntlesses produced through 1944 proved that the model was very reliable and highly successful. Navy blue with a light gray underside, the plane bore the national insignia of a dark blue circle and white star and bars outlined in blue. There was a white vertical arrow on the rudder.

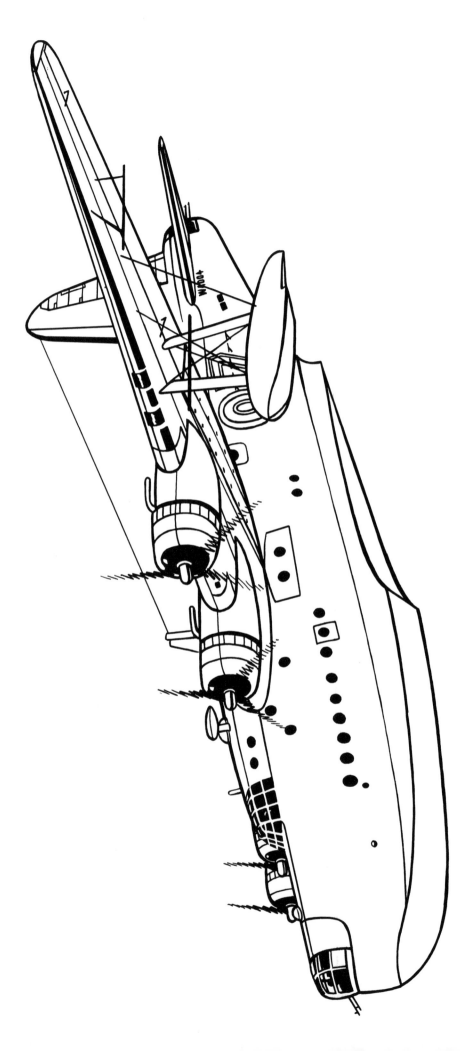

42. Short S.25 Sunderland III, 1942. Developed from the well-known Short C-class flying boat transport (it kept the C-class's double deck with crew's quarters, officers' mess, kitchen, and repair shop), the Sunderland performed excellently until the end of the war on many different RAF missions, but it was primarily a long-range sea-reconnaissance plane. In 1940 it became one of the first planes to sink a German submarine. Called "Porcupine" because of its heavy armament, over 700 of all types were built. Sea-green and dark green on top, fuselage sides and wings' undersides white, fuselage underside black. Roundel (inside to outside) red, white, blue, and yellow.

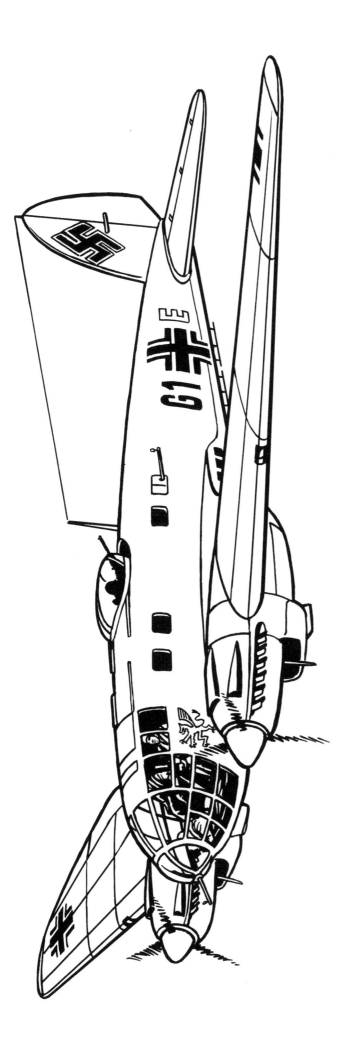

43. **Heinkel He 111H-3, 1940.** Developed in 1935 as a civilian transport, the He 111 was redesigned and became Germany's main medium bomber for the first half of the war. Many 111s bombed England before and during the Battle of Britain. Since the aircraft was not well equipped for defense, losses increased toward 1942; thus during the later war years it was used primarily as a transport. Green and dark green pattern on top, light blue underneath. Spinners yellow, letter *E* white, black swastika outlined in white, and black cross on fuselage with white and black outlines. Red lion insignia below cockpit.

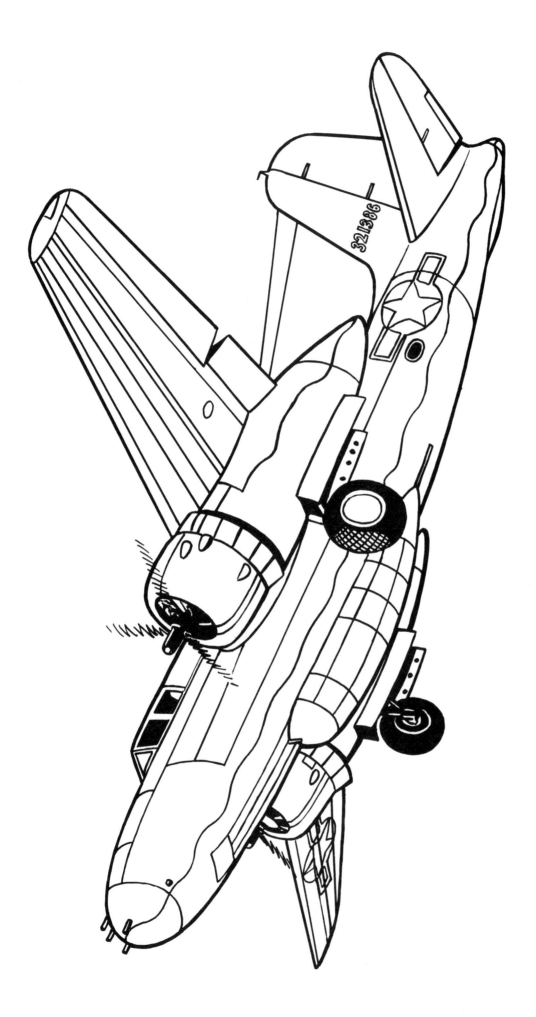

44. Douglas A-20G-40-00 Havoc. Developed from an original Douglas design of 1937 and produced for foreign countries, the Havoc was the first aircraft operated by Americans in the beginning of the war. Many Havocs went to Allied forces, including those of the Soviet Union. Besides in Europe, Havocs were employed in North Africa and the Pacific. It was primarily used as a night fighter and medium bomber. Olive drab on top, pale gray underneath. The extra jettisonable tank beneath the fuselage was white. The national insignia was a dark blue circle with a white star and bars outlined in dark blue. Rudder numerals white.

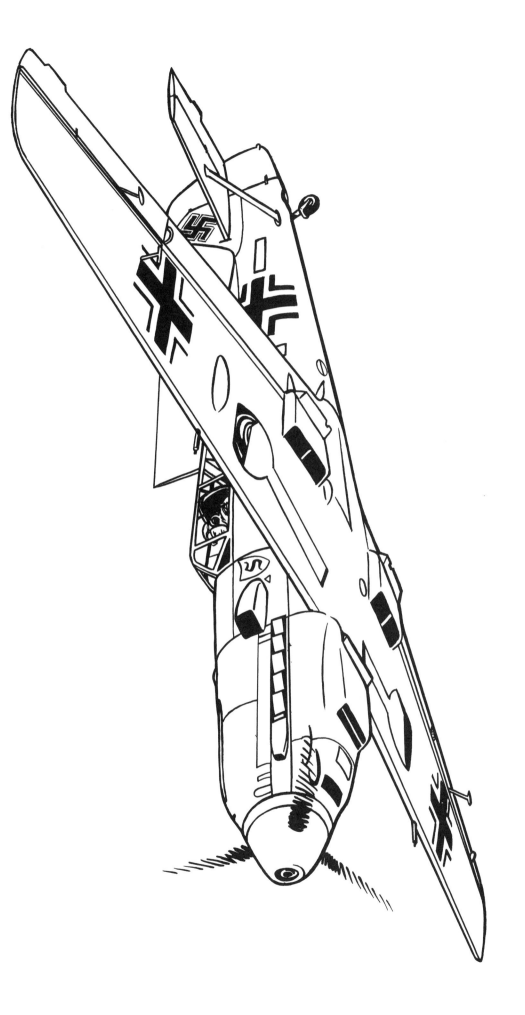

45. Messerschmitt Bf 109E-6, 1940. Developed from the civilian Bf 108, Bf 109B-1s were used in Spain during the Civil War. The 109E was employed by the German Air Force in Europe and Africa for the first three years of WWII. Termed "Emil" by its pilots, the 109E provided many German fliers with their first fighting experience. The 6th/JG26 "Schlageter," Luftflotte 2, France, was the depicted plane's squadron. Green and dark green pattern on top, fuselage sides and wings and fuselage undersides light blue. Yellow on spinner, back part of rudder, and engine cowling up to the end of the exhaust stumps. Badge white, black crosses outlined in black and white, and black swastika outlined in white.

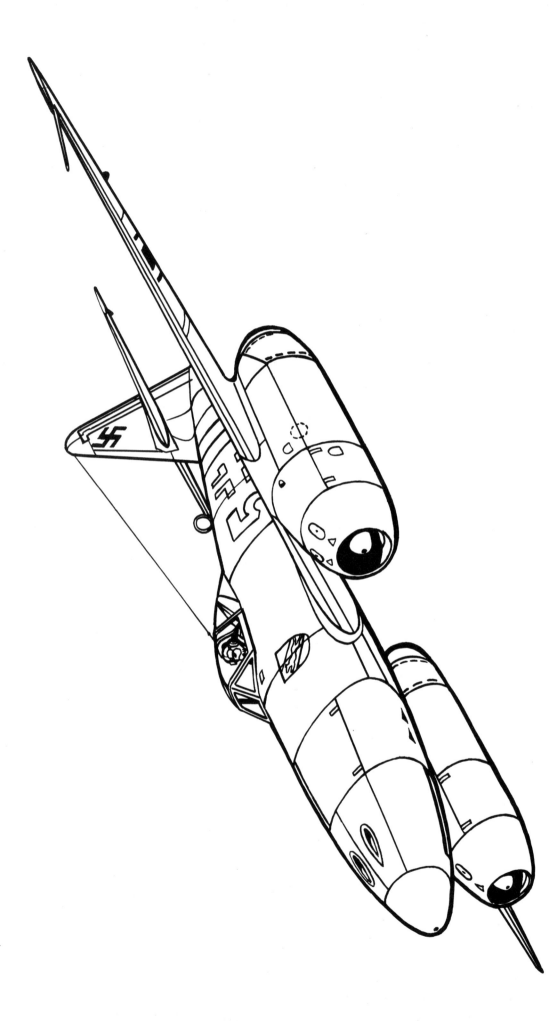

46. Messerschmitt Me 262A-1a, 1945. Called "Schwalbe" (Swallow), the 262A was introduced in May 1944 as a jet fighter, but Hitler ordered this ideal fighter to be converted into a medium bomber. He changed his mind toward the end of the war and had all Me 262s reconverted into fighters to defend Germany, but only 200 of the 400 262s were so converted by war's end. Top of fuselage and wings green with irregular dark green spots; underside light blue; top of jet engines green and dark green. Fuselage badge white with a red bar; number white; first band around back of fuselage yellow, second band white.